All About Tide Pools

All About
Tide
Pools

By Monica Halpern

NATIONAL GEOGRAPHIC

Washington, D.C.

Founded in 1888, the National Geographic Society is one of the largest nonprofit scientific and educational organizations in the world. It reaches more than 285 million people worldwide each month through its official journal, NATIONAL GEOGRAPHIC, and its four other magazines; the National Geographic Channel; television documentaries; radio programs; films; books; videos and DVDs; maps; and interactive media. National Geographic has funded more than 8,000 scientific research projects and supports an education program combating geographic illiteracy.

For more information, please call
1-800-NGS-LINE (647-5463) or write to the following address:

National Geographic Society
1145 17th Street N.W.
Washington, D.C. 20036-4688
U.S.A.

Visit us online at www.nationalgeographic.com/books

For information about special discounts for bulk purchases, please contact
National Geographic Books Special Sales at ngspecsales@ngs.org

For rights or permissions inquiries, please contact National Geographic
Books Subisidiary Rights: ngbookrights@ngs.org

Published by National Geographic Society. Washington, D.C. 20036

Design by Project Design Company
Photo Editor: Annette Kiesow
Project Editor: Anita Schwartz

Printed in the United States

Library of Congress Cataloging-in-Publication Data

Halpern, Monica.
 All about tide pools / by Monica Halpern.
  p. cm. – (National Geographic science chapters)
 ISBN 978-1-4263-0184-1 (library)
1. Tide pool ecology–Juvenile literature.
2. Tide pools–Juvenile literature. I. Title.
QH541.5.S35H35 2007
577.69'9–dc22

2007007907

Photo Credits
Front Cover: © Galen Rowell/CORBIS; Spine, Endpaper: © Raymond Gehman/CORBIS; 2-3: © Tariq Dajani/Getty Images; 6: © Wolfgang Kaehler/CORBIS; 8, 9: © Natural Sciences Image Library; 10: © Jim Richardson/CORBIS; 11, 13, 15, 26, 27, 32-33: © Shutterstock; 12 (top): © Wayne Lawler/Auscape; 12 (inset): © Kelvin Aitken/antphoto.com.au; 14: © image100/Corbis; 16, 18-19: © Kelvin Aitken/Marine Themes; 18 (inset): © Minden Pictures; 20: © Robert Yin/CORBIS; 21: © Brandon D. Cole/CORBIS; 22: © Kerrie Ruth/Auscape; 24: © Stuart Westmorland/CORBIS; 25: © Alex L. Fradkin/Getty Images; 28: © Joel Sartore/NGS/Getty Images; 30: © George D. Lepp/CORBIS; 31: © Stephen Sharnoff/National Geographic Image Collection; 35: © Jim Sugar/CORBIS.

Endsheets: A tide pool full of mussels, periwinkles, and rockweed.

Contents

Tide pools form along rocky shores. Tide pools can be large and deep or small and shallow.

What Is a Tide Pool?

The land at the edge of the ocean is called the seashore. Each day, ocean waters move onto and away from the shore. The regular rise and fall of ocean waters on the seashore is called the tide.

When the tide is high, water rushes in. Much of the seashore is covered with water. When the tide is low, or out, water moves away from the shore.

As the tide moves out to sea from a rocky shore, it leaves behind small pools of water. These pools of water are called tide pools. Tide pools are home to many different plants and animals.

At low tide, pools of seawater are left behind, on, and between the rocks.

Imagine you are walking along a rocky shore. The tide is out. All around you are little pools of water along the rocks. Kneel down and take a close look. See if you can see any plants or animals.

At high tide, seawater floods low-lying rocky areas. On most seashores, the tides are high and low twice a day.

Later, when the tide is high, seawater rushes in and covers the tide pools. The seawater carries scraps of food and oxygen. Plants and animals in the tide pools need these things to live.

A girl explores a tide pool in
British Columbia, Canada.

Chapter 1

Animals in a Tide Pool

At first you may not see many of the animals in the tide pool. You probably expect the animals to be moving around. But in tide pools, the animals stay in one place most of the time.

Look closely. Many tide pool animals attach themselves to rocks. Some have suction cups to help them hold on. Others can dig themselves into the sand. Why? So they don't wash away with the tide.

When underwater, mussels open their shells and pump water inside.

▲ Barnacles attach themselves to rocks, shells, wood, and other hard surfaces.

▲ A barnacle uses its feathery legs to sweep food into its mouth.

Do you see what look like white stones stuck to the rocks? These are barnacles. They are soft, slimy animals that live inside shells. If you are around when the tide starts to go out, you can hear the barnacles clicking their shells shut. They do this while their shells are still full of water. This water keeps them wet until the tide comes in again.

A red rock crab grabs bits of food with it pincers.

When the tide comes in, the barnacle opens up. Then, its waving legs grab bits of food floating by.

Crabs are tide pool scavengers. They eat almost anything they can find. Crabs have big front claws called pincers. Crabs use their pincers for grabbing food, walking, digging, and fighting. If a crab's claw breaks off, a new one grows in its place.

The hermit crab has tentacles, front claws, and a hard covering only on its front. It uses its back legs to hang onto the inside of a shell.

See that snail shell moving quickly along the tide pool floor? It's moving awfully fast for a snail. That's because it's not a snail. It's a hermit crab living in a snail shell. Unlike other crabs, hermit crabs have no hard shell to protect their soft body. They use empty snail shells for protection.

Did You Know?

Because the hermit crab keeps growing, it often has to find a bigger shell to live in.

A sea anemone has a "mouth" surrounded by colorful tentacles and a tubelike body. It releases a sticky substance that lets it fasten itself to a rock or shell.

If you look down through the water in some tide pools, you can see what look like beautiful flowers. But they are actually animals called sea anemones. Anemones have stinging tentacles. The anemone stings its prey and then pulls it into its mouth.

There are many kinds, shapes, and colors of seaweed. The most common along rocky shores are green, brown, and red seaweed.

Chapter 2

Plants in a Tide Pool

The plants living in a tide pool will surprise you. They don't look or feel like the plants in your home or yard. Some of the plants are slippery and slimy. Others look like lace. Some are hollow, or empty inside. Some have knots.

Most of the plants living in seawater are called algae. They are simple plants. They do not have roots, stems, leaves, or flowers. Most algae are tiny, delicate threads, but some are big with leaflike blades. The kinds of algae that live along the shore and in tide pools are called seaweed.

◄ Kelp are tough and rubbery
  plants that often grow
  where the water is cold.

   Seaweed grows on rocks, along the shore,
and in shallow water. Many float around in the
water. Like land plants, they use the energy
from sunlight to make food for themselves.
While making food, they give off the oxygen
that tide pool animals need to stay alive.

Light and thin, green seaweed bends and sways in shallow waters.

Plants are homes for many animals, too. They are safe hiding places for two important reasons. At low tide, many tide pool animals move under seaweed. Even when seaweed are out of the water, they stay wet. So, creatures living under them stay wet, too. Also, small animals hiding under seaweed are safe from other fish and hungry birds that want to eat them.

The plants in the tide pool are food for the animals that live there. Some animals eat tiny plants right off the backs of fish. Small sea snails and other animals with tongues scrape the seaweed off the rocks.

Most sea snails have a single spiral shell and a rough, zipperlike tongue they use to scrape food off the rocks.

Sea urchins feed mainly on kelp and other seaweed.

Did You Know?

Algae have many uses. Some kinds of algae are used to make food. People use seaweed in soup, sushi, and other dishes.

Chapter 3

Survival in a Tide Pool

A tide pool changes all the time. Waves crash back and forth. Water levels go up and come down. To survive high and low tides, living things in a tide pool must adapt to constant change.

Think of a day at the seashore. Winds blow. Waves pound against the shore. The plants and animals in the tide pool must hang on tightly. Otherwise, they might be tossed around or washed out to sea.

◀ As waves pound against the rocky shore, tide pool animals and plants have to keep from getting crushed or carried out to sea.

Animals use many different ways to hang on. Some snails cling to rocks with their one large foot. The foot works like a suction cup. Sea stars have tiny tube feet that help them hang onto the rocks. Mussels tie themselves to the rocks with sticky threads. Clams dig deep into the sand. Barnacles cement themselves tightly to rocks.

Mussels produce thin, sticky threads that are strong enough to keep them glued to the rocks during a storm.

At low tide, or if the water is too warm, anemones pull in their tentacles and close up to keep wet and cool inside.

Plants protect themselves during storms, too. Many plants bend and sway, but don't break. Others are glued to one spot by holdfasts. Holdfasts look something like roots, but they are not roots. They keep the plant from being washed away or torn apart.

Animals have also found ways to survive when the water is low. Clams and mussels snap their shells tightly closed to trap the water inside. Sea anemones pull in their tentacles and turn into round blobs. Shrimp, crabs, and fish hide in thick clumps of damp seaweed.

Small shrimp live mostly underwater in the moist mud.

Colorful sea stars, most with spiny skins, can be found on many seashores.

Did You Know?

Sea stars live together on the floors of tide pools. With their five arms, they look like stars. If a sea star loses an arm, it can grow another one in its place.

Chapter 4

How to Explore a Tide Pool

Plants and animals living in a tide pool have all they need to survive. They have water. They have rocks. And they have other plants and animals.

Look at the sea star and chitons in the picture. Chitons are animals. They cling to rocks. At high tide, they open their shells and eat algae. The sea star sucks in water at high tide. When the tide rolls out, it creeps across the rock. It climbs on a chiton and pulls apart the shells. Then it eats the chiton.

◀ Green sea urchins, black and white chitons, and a sea star share a tide pool in the Aleutian Islands of Alaska.

This close-up shows the eight overlapping plates on a chiton's shell.

The sea star and chitons get everything they need in the tide pool. Without the rock, seawater, and other living things, the sea star and chiton could not survive.

Sometimes, it is hard to tell if a plant or animal in a tide pool is still alive. Did it survive the crashing waves? Was it left high and dry when the tide went out?

Look for clues as you study the animals.
A living mussel holds on tight to the rock.
At low tide, its shell is closed. The shell of
a dead mussel is wide open.

Check the color of the living plants. Living
seaweed have color, often green, and are wet.
Dead seaweed are black and dry.

When exploring tide pools, move seaweed carefully to look
for animals underneath.

Tide pools are fun places to explore. But before you head out to the seashore, plan ahead. Ask an adult to go with you. Don't go off alone.

You'll want to explore during low tide. So check the times for high tides and low tides.

A group of beachcombers explore tide pools at low tide.

They are usually listed in the weather section of the local newspaper. You can find them online, too. Wear shoes that won't slip on the rocks. You may also want to take along a notebook and pencil to write about or draw what you see.

When you go exploring, be careful. You do not want to harm the living things. And you want to stay safe, too.

Here are some tips to help you explore a tide pool near you.

Tips for Exploring

★ Explore when the weather is calm, not stormy.

★ Be careful near the water. Watch out for the incoming tide.

★ Walk carefully on the rocks. Wet seaweed can be slippery.

★ Watch out for any sharp or stinging animals.

★ Be very gentle. Never take away or harm any living creature.

Children gently hold and examine sea creatures from a tide pool in Monterey Bay, California.

How to Write an A+ Report

1. Choose a topic.

- Find something that interests you.
- Make sure it is not too big or too small.

2. Find sources.

- Ask your librarian for help.
- Use many different sources: books, magazine articles, and Web sites.

3. Gather information.

- Take notes. Write down the big ideas and interesting details.
- Use your own words.

4. Organize information.

- Sort your notes into groups that make sense.

- Make an outline. Put your groups of notes in the order you want to write your report.

5. Write your report.

- Write an introduction that tells what the report is about.

- Use your outline and notes as you write to make sure you say everything you want to say in the order you want to say it.

- Write an ending that tells about your report.

- Write a title.

6. Revise and edit your report.

- Read your report to make sure it makes sense.

- Read it again to check spelling, punctuation, and grammar.

7. Hand in your report!

Glossary

adapt	to change in order to survive
algae	plants that live in the water and have no roots, leaves, or stems
coast	land along the ocean; seashore
kelp	a large, tough, brown seaweed
oxygen	a gas that is part of the air we breathe
prey	an animal hunted or caught for food
scavenger	an animal that feeds on dead and decaying plants and animals
seaweed	a type of algae that grows in seawater
tentacle	a long, thin feeler a sea animal uses to touch, hold, or move
tide	the regular rise and fall of ocean waters onto and away from the seashore
tide pool	a small pool of water left along a rocky shore at low tide

Further Reading

• Books •

Brenner, Barbara. *One Small Place By the Sea*. New York: Harper Collins, 2004. Grades 2–4, 32 pages.

Bredeson, Carmen. *Tide Pools* (First Books Series). New York: Franklin Watts, 1999. Grades 3–6, 64 pages.

Crossingham, John, and Bobbie Kalman. *Seashore Food Chains*. New York: Crabtree Publishing Company, 2005. Grades 2–4, 32 pages.

National Geographic. *My First Pocket Guide: Seashore Life*. Washington, D.C.: National Geographic Society, 2002. Grades 1–5, 80 pages.

• Web Sites •

California Department of Fish and Game
www.dfg.ca.gov/watchable/tidepools.html

Public Broadcasting Corporation (PBS)
www.pbs.org/wnet/nature/edgeofsea

San Diego Natural History Museum
www.sdnhm.org/fieldguide/places/tidepooling.html

Tides High and Low
www.saltwatertides.com

Washington State University
www.beachwatchers.wsu.edu/beaches/beachwalk

Index

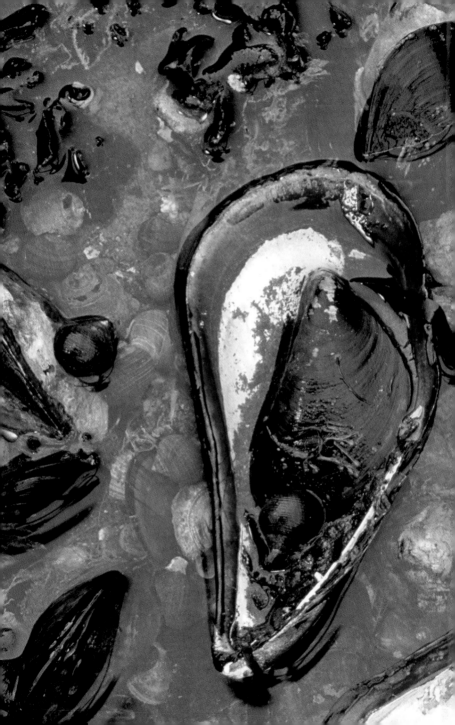